In the Still of
the Wee Morning Hours…

I FIND GOD Everywhere

(A Reverend's Musings)

Rev. Vickie L. Hughes

Lady V Publishing

© 2019 Vickie L. Hughes

All rights reserved. No part of this book may be reproduced in any form or by any electronic or mechanical means, including information storage and retrieval systems, with or without permission from the publisher or author, except in the case of a reviewer, who may quote brief passages embodied in critical articles or in a review.

Some names and identifying details have been altered to protect individual privacy.

Image by
Austin Neill / Unsplash

Cover Design by
Virtual Illustrations

Book Design by
Lady V Publishing

Acknowledgements

I thank God, *first and foremost*, for not only gifting me with a God-given writing talent but also for calling "*me*" into Ministry. I've been '*saved*' since I was a teenager; but, there came a time in my adult life when God chose to step in and save me from *myself*. My life has been right ever since I learned to get out of the way and let *God* be *God*.

Thank you to my wonderful parents; God definitely blessed me with the *right ones* who have supported me through *thick and thin*. I started writing at the young age of 16; I've never stopped. That was 40 years ago! Writing has always given me life, especially when I was shy in my younger years. I know that my parents, and other folks I know (including myself… Hehe…), have been waiting for me to publish a book for decades since that's been a dream of mine for over 30 years; finally, the time is here after prior attempts that came with issues such as limited time and distractions due to educational/career pursuits, computer viruses, outdated disks, and warped flash drives. Whew! After this book, there are more to come. Last Christmas, I got a pleasant surprise when I learned that my young niece, who is now 12 years old (my one and only biological niece), has also started writing early in life. I hope and pray that she will continue to do so. *"Sophia, I love you with my whole heart and then some."*

Thank you to the numerous professors who *believed* in me. Thank you to those individuals who have *encouraged* me to keep pushing and thriving, during times of trials and tribulations. Thank you to my current Pastor, Rev. Jordan B. Boyd (Senior Pastor, Rockwell AME Zion Church, Charlotte, NC), who reminds me *often* to trust God *completely* and *allow* Him to "*do the rest.*" Much love to my Church family at Rockwell, where I serve as an Ordained Deacon on the Ministerial Team.

I love everybody who has ever crossed my path whether you have remained in my life or *not*, because you have either *shown me love* and/or taught me some of *life's* lessons. Love you all! I wish you many blessings in your remaining lives.

Foreword

I first met Rev. Vickie Hughes, while she was a student in my seminary class. I enjoyed having Vickie as a student; as her professor, I also learned from her life experiences. Even now, many years later, I am still learning from Vickie. She remains a bright shining star, a beacon of hope, and a voice worth listening to.
I am proud to see Vickie graduate from seminary and venture into the world sharing her God-given gifts with the larger community.

Vickie shares inspirational discoveries in her new book, *"In the Still of the Night and the Wee Morning Hours... I FIND GOD EVERYWHERE."* Her personal journey as a daughter, aunt, attorney, congregational pastor, and hospital chaplain to name a few, have shaped her interactions with countless people of various backgrounds on her journey. Vickie lets us in on her journey, specifically her personal spiritual awakenings amid pain, joy, confusion, and other life experiences.

Millions of people find meaning while participating in activities attended by large crowds. In fact, often an intoxicating energy can be detected in crowds of people. Large crowds can be experienced while attending worship services, concerts, athletic events, self-help activities, and other gatherings. Of course, there are some people who avoid crowds, feeling overwhelmed and out of place. Nonetheless, large facilities are constantly being built across the world to accommodate growing crowds to gather for athletic teams, religious events, and other activities. Yet in her book, Vickie shows the reader that there can be significance and transformation in private moments away from large crowds of people, alone with God.

In todays' world, billions of people pursue a connection to digital communities using Facebook, Twitter, Instagram, YouTube, and other platforms. Vickie describes fulfilling spiritual encounters without using computers, the internet, or electronic devices. I am glad that Vickie does not restrict God to a certain orthodoxy(s) and location(s). I'm thankful that God does not need electricity or other modern devices to communicate love and grace to us. She gives wonderful examples of God's presence in unexpected places and unanticipated spaces. Let us follow Vickie's examples in this captivating book and share with others, her stories and our own, as we value and exhibit listening and learning from one another.

Grace and Peace,

Ken J. Walden, Ph.D.
President-Dean, Gammon Theological Seminary
(Author of the following three books: *Practical Theology for Church Diversity; Challenges Faced by Iraq War Reservists and Their Families; A Pastor's Poetry: Volume One*)

Preface

If it had not been for the Lord on my side...

"Quiet INTROSPECTION of the Divine"

In the still of the night and the wee morning hours... I find God everywhere! I often find Him in the most unlikely places. It is then when He's at His loudest, although a whispering presence. During some slumbering moments over the years, I've awakened to hear His voice. He silently speaks to me and through me as my pen glides across pages of paper. Often, I stop dead in my tracks in the midday hours. But then, I'm alone with Him again at night. He aids me in retracing my steps while in deep reflection. Put another way, His silence speaks! I quickly find some paper and write what He gives me in sacred, comforting moments.

My God is everything! He walks with me and He talks with me. He protects me and He guides me! He is my refuge in times of trouble and my Savior when I need Him most.

God never fails me, even when my behavior has been less than desirable. He sticks with me, waiting for me to recognize and correct my wrongdoing. God is patient with me, when He needs me to learn the lessons He has set in motion for me to catch. And He gets my attention when He wants to impart His wisdom on me, so that I can preach and teach to others whom He has strategically placed in my path... *God and I travel down this road called life together.* We are partners and confidantes! I've had quite the journey. God empowers me and I pay that forward.

"My Ministerial Life after Seminary"

When I was younger, I loved writing during the wee hours of the morning. As I've aged, my insight has shifted. *I truly believe that in the still of the night and the wee morning hours is when/where I experience God and find Him at work the most.* It is *so* fitting that He called *me* into Ministry; yet, I am *humbled*. In recent years, I have worked in a Chaplain *capacity* as both a Resident and as an Intern at three different healthcare locations; this Fall I hope to secure a full-time Chaplain job in a healthcare facility or a college/university setting. I absolutely loved working night on calls while ministering to patients and their loved ones. There have been times when I've been in patients' rooms in the middle of the night because their pain has been so great, that they couldn't sleep. Some nights, deaths have occurred, and I have walked to various units/floors to comfort families. Lonely people seem to be the loneliest at night; I've been there with them to listen, talk, and/or pray. There have been medical personnel on duty who are away from their families; I have often encountered them as we share a kind word or a laugh or two. God *is* everywhere! And He *especially* shows up in places like hospitals where many of His people are ill, often critically; these individuals are *desperately* fighting for their lives. This is when God *powerfully* shows up and often shows out! He sometimes proves physicians wrong, because He is the ultimate Doctor and has the *final* say. God sticks by those individuals who are deathly ill and sends people like me to interact with their families. God *speaks through certain people* to comfort other people; God has called *me* to be *one* of those people. Traumas *change* people! They get sad, they get angry, they get confused, and/or worried. They run the gamut of emotions, but God is *always* there for them, through it all. God *always* appears in *some* way; He *makes* His presence *known*! I've seen patients in an Intensive Care Unit go to a step-down floor, rehabilitation center, and home from there. Many of the patients I have referenced have arrived at the healthcare facility with life-threatening injuries. Some are not expected to live, others are not expected to walk and talk again; yet, God gives many of these same individuals another chance to live again. He may, however, expect them to live differently now. He spares their lives for this reason, providing them another route to fulfilling their earthly destinies/callings/assignments. God has specific plans for and in His Kingdom; we all play a role in it.

"A Reminiscent Moment"

Just sitting and waiting for dinner at one of my favorite restaurants... *Reminiscing...*

I'm remembering how *Jesus didn't just save my life*; He *saved me* from *myself*. God had been tugging at me for years. I was busy chasing what I thought I was supposed to chase... A career, success, and whatever else. That all came to a halt when I left a high-paying job, unbelievable benefits, autonomy, and a satisfying, amazing life in Phoenix, to attend law school in another State. After law school, my legal career pursuit was a disaster, in my opinion, with some unexpected trying times! It was that time in the wilderness when God stepped in. And *this* time, God was not tugging or nudging; He was *boldly* calling. And trust me when I tell you that, *"I answered."*

If it had not been for the Lord on my side… "Where, oh where, would I be?"

I'm not sure how much longer I'll be on this earth, but... There is something that I know *for sure*... I know that Ministry is right for me, whatever that looks like with God's guidance and direction. I'm excited to see how God will position me/use me in Ministry next. And I wonder where I'll be living, who will befriend me, which man I might be dating, where I might travel, who might invite me to preach/speak, and what my life will look like. My future awaits, and *I am here for it*!

There is *one thing* that I know for sure *about the world* we know today… I have discovered that there are numerous individuals across our Country and around the world who are hurting, who crave attention, who desire that displays of dignity are shown to them/others, who search for meaning/purpose, and who need love. As someone personally and professionally groomed for leadership roles, I speak with "pastoral authority." God called me into ministry many years ago. While my calling was initially unclear, I am now an ordained minister serving in a Chaplain/Preacher/Devotion Leader capacity. I preach, I teach, I motivate, I empower, I inspire! As a person educationally prepared for psychology, law, and ministry... I care about people, so I also empathize and comfort. This book is written and shared with a certain audience in mind; it is specifically geared toward those individuals who desperately *want* to and *need* to hear from God, whether they are in some sort of Ministerial role or not. It will also appeal to those individuals who need a *reminder* of God's goodness during trying times.

In my book, you'll find sacred moments, situational prayers, reflective thoughts, spiritual quotes, inspirational messages, profound sermons, and more. Enjoy these spiritual/theological reflections *(this Reverend's musings)* written along my life's journey; I've chosen to share them with you. No more mask wearing… Meet the raw, vulnerable "*me*." Turn the pages and experience what God has to say to you, through me. May God richly bless each and every one of you. *Thank you so much for your support!*

Rev. Vickie L. Hughes
Summer 2019

REVERENCE

"I Dedicate This Poem to You, Lord"

You gave me the will to live;
You even saved me from death.
You pulled me away from trouble;
You helped me to see the light.
You encouraged me and gave me reasons to love myself;
because You did,
I am ecstatic that You've been a major part of my life…
Who am I fooling?
You *have been* and *are* my life.
It is time for me to confess to the world,
that I love You.

"MY Personal Messages to the Public"

"I *know* that God is *so* amazing. He has shown that He can, through other people, do any and everything to bless me... Even when I have least expected it, blessings have come in a mighty way. I remain grateful and humble. What God can do for *me*, He can do for *you*! Have strong faith and *expect* the unexpected. Blessings will come pouring in and when they do... Praise Him!"

"I, Rev. Vickie L. Hughes, am thankful for my love affair with Jesus. And *this* is...
'*Not* an *ordinary* love!'
Lord, I just keep *falling* for You...
Yes, Lord... I just keep *falling* for You."

"MY God"

My God...
You bring me joy,
when I am down.
I've learned to pray,
without making a sound.
You lift me up when I fall;
all I have to do is call.

You are *my* God!
You present no facade.
Some may find that odd!
You want others to know who You are,
so You encourage
Your family of Christians
not to stray very far.
If Your light so shines
in them,
everyone will see
that the trials that they face in life,
are only *temporarily* dim.

I trust in You, Lord.
You are my shield and sword.
As I engage in inner reflection,
I consider this next section...

If hope abides in all,
our blessings won't stall...
Favor will surface
once things happening behind the scenes,
are put in place.

God, You work at Your own pace.

When humanity
comes to know You intimately,
we start to praise You fervently.
God, You deserve recognition;
You are the one who brings
great things into fruition.

Uniting our hearts to Yours
giving our whole selves,
reciprocal effects occur.
As our lives fuel up
and fill up with Your love,
others will see
a change in us.
The peace that
resides in many of us,
we shall share with others
and often discuss.

As I center my thoughts,
directly back to You, O God,
I give You honor and praise...
That's a huge nod!

Lord, You are *my* God;
You are who protects me from harm,
sounds my internal alarm,
guides my path,
and redirects wrath.
You are forever *my* love
as You watch over me;

You navigate from above.

I praise Your name.
You are a constant in *my* life;
You are always here for me.
As the world swirls around me
with all of its twists and turns,
You are always within reach...
You never change.

I thank You, God,
for who You are.
I find comfort
in knowing that
no matter what,
I can call on You... You aren't very far.
I find comfort in knowing,
Your omnipresence
is mind-blowing.
Your glory, Lord,
is Your badge of honor.
Teach and show creation,
these things, O God,
so that
we are always knowing...
Please keep Your blessings overflowing. Amen.

A Devotion: "Resting Place"

We go through
so much,
as we live this life.
Curveballs are
thrown at us,
causing us to worry.
Sometimes,
we have deadlines
causing us to hurry.
We have obligations
to fulfill.
Each day, there will be
things to do,
people to see,
and places to be.
Our days are full
of busyness,
of hectic tasks.
At some point,
we *must* slow down.
We *must* refuel
so that we get that second wind,
and carry on.
We come here
during the week,
because *this* is
our resting place.
It is here in this Chapel,
where we can exhale
and release.
We can love others.

We can pray.
Reflecting on life,
we acknowledge
our blessings.
We wish others well.
Words such as healing,
grace, and mercy,
are mentioned.
Tension melts away.
Refreshed and renewed,
we can continue on,
with the day.
Yes,
This is
our resting place.
Pausing us
and redirecting us
as needed,
from those daily trying difficulties,
and stressful interactions,
we face.

(PRAYER time!)

Let us recognize our blessings,
silently expressing gratitude.
Let us then take the time
to pray for others,
in need of mercy and grace. (PAUSE)

*If there are prayer requests at this time,
make them known silently or publicly now.* (PAUSE)

Let us pray:
Father God, as we gather here today, we thank You for our blessings. Thank You for waking us up this morning. We are here in this resting place right now, lifting up others who need You right now. Provide comfort where it is needed. Ease pain when people are crying out. Father, You know the needs of people we've encountered and those we've never met. Whatever Your will is today, let it be done. Amen.

"A Mother's Day Tribute
from a child's viewpoint/reflection
(an ode to my mother, Evelyn B. Hughes)"
May 12, 2019

In the beginning,
before I was formed...
God had partnered with my mother,
to bring about another creation...
Me, moi.
Woosah!
Actively growing,
as my seed was sowing...
This fact was physically evident,
my mother was ever-knowing.

I found myself in my mother's womb.
Exploration was the name of the game;
survival, of utmost concern.
Skills acquired there before birth,
helped me later in life I'd learn.
I discovered early,
how to navigate on this earth.

I was to be the first-born,
a title upon my birth I'd earn.
The example
(and a little child shall lead them),
the guinea pig,
the experiment,
the role model;
the little girl with an inner child,
that they would coddle.

Trial and error,
I was never a "holy terror."
Occasionally rebellious yes;
there *were* times when I was a mess.
Strictness and discipline,
awaited me then.
I'd straighten up quickly.
Reflecting back on those days,
I vividly remember,
lessons learned "thickly."
I laugh because,
those things helped me to knowingly,
change my path.
I *never* welcomed wrath.

Train up a child,
in the way that she should go;
when that child gets old,
she will not depart from those words,
her mother used to say.
As the years have gone by...
Regrets and memories
of mistakes/wrong choices,
have sometimes made me cry.
But in my life,
joys have always,
outweighed the pains.
Trials have bred gains.

At times over the years,
in the midst of tears,
an answer has followed a "why."

My mother and I
have shared in my disappointments;
but then,
"changed" courses have come,
in the form of strong, God-given hints.
Pleasantly surprised,
we've been able to smile again.

I've always hoped,
to make my mother proud.
There have been times when,
my accomplishments
have spoken pretty loud.
In those moments...
I've looked to the hills,
focused on one
amazingly big cloud,
and praised God
for getting me through,
for guiding me along,
for providing me wisdom,
for protecting me from harm,
and for blessing me,
with favor and grace.

I would be remiss
if I didn't give my mother credit,
for cheering me on
and motivating me each time,
until I've reached a finish line.
She's a gem!
I've always had her *and* Him
(aka *my* God),

by my side.
Their love for me,
they could never hide.

Now, as for me,
my mother's child...
Forever achieving is what I've known.
Sowing seeds of greatness,
so that I've always grown.
I, like my mother,
have in my adult journey,
some historic firsts.
Lifelong learners,
knowledge thirsts.

I have inherited her creative ways;
I am carrying on her caring nature.
This is something I know,
for sure.

One day decades later, after my birth...
I realized that
I'd found God in myself
(my mother now knows);
and that,
I'd evolved into
an even better person.
I'd discovered the essence of
who I was and who I am,
a favored "being" led by the One.
He's who I'll worship and praise,
all of my days!

What began as my mother's desire
to bear a child in
and of the genetics of thee,
evolved and transformed
into a "God calling" in the form of "me."
Thank you to my mother for,
desiring motherhood.
God understood;
and then,
I came to be.

BLESSED ASSURANCE

"God"

God is on my side,
nowhere can I hide.
He is always there for me.
He helps me to see,
things I never saw before.
He shows me right from wrong;
He even teaches me how to be strong.

"Morning Has Spoken"

Every day I see His face.
I remember His grace.
I seek His approval;
I love His style.
I don't want to please Him every once in awhile;
but rather, all of the time.
My love for Him is sublime.

He lets me know that He knows my every move…
He also *delves deep* into my thoughts.
I welcome His presence,
within me.
He's my awesome God you see,
and He will always be.

"He's All I Need"

Yes,
He died for me!
Jesus has a special place in my heart.
Daily, I count on Him because He's there for me as He does His part…
He protects me.
He shows me righteous living.
He guides me.
He imparts His wisdom on me.
He never leaves me alone.
He loves me.

There's a story here. Let's see -
Where do I start?
Well… He didn't have to beg.
He didn't have to knock.
I just invited Him in.

One day, He asked me,
"Would you be my wife?"
Long ago, I said, "Yes."
Each day, He continues to bless.
He carries me,
when my life rages like a stormy sea.
Then,
after awhile things are fine.
He's so powerful.
He can change a life.
So glad, He happened in mine.

I urge you to call on Him,
when you need a friend.
He will walk alongside you
and sometimes even carry you,
until the end.

"His Silence Speaks"

His silence speaks…
I hear it during certain hours,
when He knows that
my mind has quieted down.

Sometimes,
He diverts my attention,
to a beautiful nature scene.
It is there where I glean,
His amazing being.
There are times when something happens
like an unexpected blessing;
I can sense and know that it's Him.

A person
may say something
and it sounds like something that,
God would say.
Often, I hear His words,
or see signs of God's presence.
He just shows up when I believe that,
I am alone.
From time to time,
He appears to me
while I'm surrounded by a sea of people.

God never leaves me absent,
without His presence.
His silence speaks ever so *loudly*,
at times.

His awesomeness,
often overwhelms me…
Whenever I ponder God's goodness,
scenes come to the surface;
they flash before my eyes.
I am awestruck *right* then.
I know how giving and faithful He's been.
I can honestly say that concerning God's vastness,
my mind's blown.
His silence speaks;
His voice is all I've ever known.

"Still Rising"

On this day,
we remember Jesus.
He was
never bitter
toward those who,
mistreated and
abused Him.
He didn't stay
in His tomb,
wallowing in sorrow
over the loss of His life;
what horrific acts humanity had
done to Him...
Yet, He forgave.
He wanted
to show us;
we can overcome
our obstacles,
our trials.
We can defeat
our enemies,
if we just try...
If we believe we can,
we shall.
Jesus wasn't
about to allow
defeat to win.
He was greater than *that*.
So,
He got up!

Because of Him,
we can face our tomorrows.
With His example
as our guide,
we can
overcome anything.
We can conquer
the worst of it all.
We can win!
He did it for us,
to show us that
no matter what...
Life prevails!
With each day comes,
the realization that...
Jesus lives in all of us;
He's still forgiving,
He's still loving,
He's still guiding, and
He's still walking
alongside of each of us.
With each new day,
He's still rising.
We can too!

Holy Week Sermon - Haw River United Methodist
Church, Haw River, NC
[Monday (3-26-2018)]
Guest Preacher: Rev. Vickie L. Hughes
Luke 23:32-43KJV, "Forget Me Not"

My INTRO: "Your Church's theme for this year's Holy Week remembrance is 'At the Foot of the Cross.' Tonight, we will focus on '*Forgiveness*.' Luke 23:34 includes one of Jesus's last sayings, '...*Father, forgive them; for they know not what they do...*' That saying is extremely powerful; it speaks volumes! I want to dig even deeper than that tonight. Is that okay with everyone?" *(End of Intro)*

Imagine yourselves at the foot of the Cross, near Jesus's feet. Hopefully, you took up your own crosses when you became disciples and followed Jesus. If that is the case, here you are like Mary (the sister of Martha and Lazarus) listening to Jesus intently/resting calmly at His feet, as if you are at their house. Whether you are young or old, you should be excited; there is always something new to learn from or about Jesus. Tonight, we can visualize Jesus being up on that cross; He is teaching even in His last moments of agony/of suffering. Just like He taught throughout His 3-year ministerial travels, make no mistake... Yes, He *is*, teaching humanity some lessons while hanging on that cross.

The focus for tonight is on certain words in verse 34, which let us know that Jesus is praying to God to forgive humanity for their sins. In Luke 23:34 from the King James Version (KJV), Jesus's memorable words are written as follows, *"Father, forgive them; for they know not what they do."* Many of the people He is praying for at that moment have been sinning for years. And they would not know or understand this fact or Jesus's purpose to save them from their sins, until after Jesus is long gone. The Jews had read about/heard about a coming Savior for years. Here He is, right in front of their very eyes and they have no clue. How *sad* is that!

As we read on in Luke 23, we encounter another powerful image. I want to highlight verses 39-43, detailing Jesus's interaction with 2 criminals on the crosses on either side of Him. We can find more than one lesson on forgiveness in Luke 23! One thing we've already learned about Jesus is that, He wasn't just about talking. Have you heard the term, "Walk the talk?" *Jesus* walked His talk. Here, He's asked God to forgive the Jews who persecuted Him, and then immediately demonstrates the very act of forgiveness that He's just asked God to do for the others. Unlike many of the people standing at the foot of the cross and one of the criminals, the other criminal is actually remorseful and believes that Jesus can help him in his time of need. He is about to die a slow and horrific death, and he has no idea what will become of him after that. So, he chooses to believe in Jesus and holds onto some hope. Jesus forgives the sins of this one criminal who chooses to believe in Jesus. He has taken a chance and professes his belief in front of everyone. He is obviously, genuine.

Remember, Jesus has already prayed… Father, *forgive* them! *(Let that sink in.)* Here, Jesus is, "on His death bed" let's say. And He is thinking about humanity. He is praying for us (all people), rather than Himself! Who does *that*? *Nobody but Jesus*!

Here, Jesus is in the company of two types of criminals or people in His immediate vicinity. They are way up high, as the three of them suffer on their crosses...

On one side of Jesus is a criminal or person who recognizes his wrongs and is remorseful, wanting to repent. He is promised eternal life.

On the other side, there is the other criminal or person who believes himself to be right, thinking he's done no wrong. He isn't open to even hearing what Jesus is saying or doing at the time. He isn't open to learning any of the lessons that life offers. He is going to refuse anything offered to him... He is hard-headed, stubborn, selfish, and screwed! We can probably think of some people we know like this… Perhaps ourselves!

This scenario with Jesus and the two criminals reminds me of death row. When a criminal is close to death, he or she is offered his/her last meal. If you've given up or stopped caring about any and everything, you might tell the prison guard that you don't want anything. You might have this attitude, *"Just let me die!"*

But if you regret your life and the sins you committed... You will have a glimmer of hope that, you may have a second chance to right your wrongs. You're going to order the finest things to get a taste of the good life, perhaps even what you've missed out on your entire life. You're going to order lobster, filet mignon, a baked potato, and a slice of apple pie. And how about some champagne? Do you know that many criminals find God while in prison? Why wouldn't they; don't they need some hope that their lives are going to be alright? And don't forget that in today's world, sometimes death penalty cases are stayed or reversed... Lives are extended or given chances to turn around... Actually, that is the case in other cases too, like in the lives of some terminally-ill people. Often, lives are spared or given more years on this earth. Jesus dying on that cross has given many of us that kind of hope! We can live longer than we can only imagine. Many people live long lives on earth. And we can all live eternally in heaven, if we truly believe that Jesus's crucifixion/resurrection occurred to ensure our salvation. We need to spread the Good News of that hope around.

Jesus forgave one of those criminals hanging on a cross, in His last moments; yet, in modern times such as these... We are so quick to judge people just like this. We judge ex-offenders, homeless people, and mentally ill people for what they have done or have not done. Forgive them, for they know *not* what they do! Isn't that what Jesus prayed to our Father, when people were judging *Him*?

As Christians, we know what we are doing! And if we are not forgiving people for what they have done in the past... We are *not* being *Christ-like* at all! We are actually being hypocrites, if we are calling ourselves Christians. Jesus let us know what He was about, up until He took His last breath. He exuded love and fairness. And He promoted acceptance and forgiveness. We are supposed to model His behavior.

If Jesus could forgive in His last moments, *surely*, we can forgive others too. That is what *Christianity* is all about... Forgiveness of sins, and how that forgiveness gets us to heaven to live eternally.

While He's speaking personally with God, Jesus was teaching the people a lesson on forgiveness. We must never forget that He turned and forgave one of the criminals hanging on his own cross. And then Jesus assured this criminal that he would see Jesus in heaven, because he believed. This reminds us that salvation is offered to *everyone*. It is offered to us until we take our last breaths. Some call that *"deathbed faith."* It is never too late to turn our lives around and I'm also referring to the chance at eternal life here. We can't *depend* on that though. If you're killed instantly, you may not get a *"come to Jesus"* moment. Repent *now*, if you need to!

Jesus forgave all people on God's behalf; yet, they still didn't understand His authority to do so and continued to sin. When God forgives us as a people, we need to make a conscious effort to change our behavior. He's trying to move us forward, not keep us stuck in the past or present! He's trying to further His Kingdom.

While preparing this sermon, the term, 'forget me not' popped into my head. I thought to myself, those words are so appropriate to Jesus's Crucifixion and the surrounding circumstances!

I chose to Google the significance of the Forget Me Not flower. So, *what exactly does the Forget Me Not flower represent*, according to my Google search? To my surprise, my search yielded these results:

-True and undying love
-Remembrance during partings or after death
-A connection that lasts through time
-Fidelity and loyalty in a relationship, despite separation or other challenges
-Reminders of your favorite memories or time together with another person
-Growing affection between two people
-Caring for the poor, disabled, and needy

Do these things not describe Jesus and the relationships we desire to have with Him? We should all remember the forget-me-not flower, whenever we think of Jesus. Imagine that He is here in the flesh amongst us tonight, whispering to us, *"Forget Me Not."* He would remind us that He forgave us long ago. Are we paying that forward?

Think about our interactions with each other. We could stand to forgive some people from past or current circumstances. As humans, we are good for staying mad at people... Some of us hold onto grudges for way too many years!

Never forget... Jesus forgives! Remember Jesus is like a forget-me-not flower. He paid the ultimate price for us; now we have a long-lasting relationship with Him. Jesus would say to us, "Forget me not. Remember that I forgave you long ago. Forgive that person or those persons who have wronged you. Forgiveness helps you! And while you're at it… Ask others to forgive you… Tell them that their lives depend on it!"

The lists of petitions for pardons and pleas could go on and on, for each of us. My friends, we've all been sinning for years, because we are human. Jesus knew that… He understood that! That's why He came to earth. That's why He died the way He did. He agreed to pay the price for our sins, and He did just that! I know this because like all of humanity, I was at the foot of that cross on the day Jesus was crucified. As I stood at the foot of that cross, listening and watching intently like Mary, Martha's sister, did with Jesus as He taught; I learned that Jesus forgives even the worst of us. So, as wretched as I am as a long-time sinner already forgiven by Jesus, I ask that you forgive me for all that I've done. And I forgive all of you for the unspeakable sins you've committed throughout your lives. If we all forgive others, the world will be a better place.

Jesus left us while we ("humanity") stood at the foot of that cross... He left us after having forgiven us. We must do as Jesus did; we must forgive others as He has forgiven us. We can rest calmly at Jesus's feet like Mary did at the home of Martha, Mary, and Lazarus; whenever Jesus taught. Jesus was indeed teaching, while humanity stood at the foot of that cross. Jesus asked God to forgive humanity back then, because they had no idea that they were sinning greatly. Centuries later, we know! And although already forgiven, we can always ask God for forgiveness when we sin, believing in the promise of salvation. Lord, when judgment day comes... "Forget *me* not!" Amen.

LIFE'S TRIALS AND VULNERABLE TIMES

"Death Crept Upon Us"

Death crept upon us.
It actually took one of us.
So young, so new.
"Why him?"
I'm sure that You had a purpose, Lord.
I know it was a good one.
There was no reason to put up a fuss.
Death crept upon us.
His face - So cold, so pale.
I waited for it to move,
to show signs of life... Of living!
As the coffin was closed,
I wanted to shout, "Come back!"
Instead, I cried a tear for my friend;
I cried a tear for his life snuffed out so soon.
For us, this was an unfamiliar tune,
to lose a friend so young.
Death had indeed crept upon us.

"Consumed by Loneliness or Something"

Consumed by loneliness,
I never dreamt of this.
Reflecting into the future
wanting to know for sure,
that this feeling I have
will not last until the end of time.

Consumed by emptiness,
I never dreamt of this.
Searching for fulfillment.
Wanting to be content.
Consumed by uncertainty,
while wondering why these feelings are felt by me.
Forever reaching for God's love,
looking for this to come from
up above.

Consumed by anger,
yet knowing I must erase
these thoughts,
for fear of sins of danger.

Consumed by incomplete wholeness,
I never dreamt of this.
Waiting for my heart to mend,
waiting for those things or persons that,
God plans to send.

Just waiting for the future…

"FAITH while waiting… Faith MATTERS"

"An ounce of faith can move a ton of anything!"

"If I can bless somebody else, God will bless me... *Again*... And *again*."

"Follow me to the place where God leads me. He just may have a lesson or blessing for *you*."

"I need to develop my reactions to the devil's distractions from God's timely actions!"

"Thank You, Lord, for removing those individuals from my life who had no business in it!"

"God is in the midst of every storm. The devil might be stirring things up a little, or a lot. Meanwhile, God is on the sidelines just checking things out... Just waiting for the right time to intervene, calm the waters, and make things right. Boy, we as humans can sure make a mess out of some things, can't we? Rest assured, God *is* watching."

"Shame"

The shame of it all!
Hiding behind the mask,
with its many dips and marks.
Each representation a period of life,
a specific event, or a time of hurt/rejection...
Withdrawing to go inside of my head.
It really matters what was said,
until it becomes a distant dig.
Thinning like a twig!
At different times, I've worked on me.
I leave behind the worst,
feeling positively empowered
to move forward.
My mask comes off.
I see clearer.
The shade and
the darkness I've hidden in,
as a safe place.
I've always seen His face.
I think of His goodness.
I hear His voice,
calling me closer.
He calls my name
and speaks my truth.
He gives me my next assignment...
Then, into the world I burst.

PRAYERFUL EXISTENCE

"Chaplain's Corner"

"A Chaplain's Prayer"
Holy Spirit, reign down on me. Increase my self-awareness and hone my internal work both in and out of patient visits/family interactions. Work *through* me as I empathize with others' pain, fear, and grief. Let my *tears flow* and *emotions shine*, where need be. *Replenish me* when I am drained and help me *discern* when *enough* is *enough*. Allow me to *celebrate the joy* of my success, when I have *made a connection* and *touched someone's soul* as he/she continues *fighting for* his/her life. *Strengthen* my spirit. *Shape* me, *mold* me further into that being that You've called me to *be*. *Trusting in the process*, Father God. Have *Your* way with *me*. Flow *through* me and out *to* others. Thank *You* for calling *me*. Amen.

"A PRAYER for those who are ill"
Heavenly Father, encourage us to band together as caring individuals and help others who need love right now. Show us how to be there for them. Guide us to the people who need us more. Give us the words to say or actions to do, so that You shine through us and lift others' spirits. For those fighting for their lives or those hurting from physical, mental, or emotional pain... Help us to wrap our arms around them. Help us, help them. Father, thank You for Your guiding light. And thank You for this season of hope, faith, miracles, grace, joy, family, forgiveness, and love. Amen.

"A PRAYER for someone having surgery"
Lord, I'm here with this patient, one of Your children. Thank You for surrounding him/her with loved ones while he/she is here at the hospital. As You know, this patient will be having surgery soon. This patient is feeling anxious about his/her hospital stay and his/her upcoming surgery. Ease his/her anxiety, Lord. Wrap Your arms around this patient and make Your presence known. He's/she's one of Your children. Show Your love to this patient at this time, Father. And steady the surgeon's hands as You guide them through this patient's surgery. I pray for a successful surgery. Father, thank You for Your love. We thank You for waking all of us up this morning. Thank You for Your grace and mercy. Father, please allow this patient to know when his/her surgery will be and allow it to happen soon, so that he/she won't be so anxious. Calm this patient's nerves. Help him/her to rest and relax. I ask these things in Your name, Lord. Amen.

"A PRAYER for those in need of tender loving care"
Loving God, I pray for those who are mentally ill and emotionally lonely. May You, God, wrap Your arms around them and let them know that You will always be there for them. As they are tormented, turn their troubled thoughts into pleasant ones. When they think of ending their lives believing that no one cares, walk with them as their 'friend' so that they know that they have a friend in You. Provide them with a hedge of protection. I ask these things in Your mighty name, Lord. Amen.

"A PRAYER for someone who wants to give up, someone contemplating suicide"

Creator God, I don't know how much longer I can go on. I need You more than ever now. I've thought about ending my life. My existence here on earth has caused so much strife. I keep losing my footing… One step forward, two steps back! I feel so worthless. Help me, God. I'm crying out for help! I want my life to have meaning; but right now, I don't know my purpose. I'm just wading through life. I'm existing. Nothing has worked out right. Father, help me save my life. I desperately ask this in Your name. Amen.

"A PRAYER for a better, improved life"

Lord, I am in need of a blessing or two right now. You know what I need. I can't support my family without a good job. I can't live right if I don't have a roof over my head. I'm stressed just trying to make it every day. Lord, help me figure out how to better my life. My life is a mess! I don't know why I'm going through hard times right now, Lord. I need Your help. Hear my prayer, O Lord. Amen.

"A PRAYER for someone battling addiction"

Holy Spirit, I call on You now. My addiction is killing my family and me. I've been addicted for so long. I can't seem to stop on my own. The verse, Philippians 4:13, says that "I can do all things through Christ which strengthens me." After numerous attempts at quitting, I haven't been able to quit on my own. I am weak, Lord. I need Your help. Guide me. Help me to replace my bad habits with productive activities. I want to live! Right now, I've hit rock bottom. I want to do better. Save my life, Lord. I want to live! Help me quit this addiction for my family's sake and mine, Lord. Amen.

"A PRAYER for a person being abused"
Father God, I can't take this abuse anymore. I'm scared that he/she is going to kill me. I'm in fear of my life every day. I know that I don't deserve to be treated this way, but I don't know how to get away from him/her. Help me come up with a support plan. Direct me to the proper resources. Give me reasons to feel good about myself. I want to be loved, not hurt. Father, I have put up with this abuse for so long. He/she isolated me from my family and friends, so I have nowhere to turn but to You. Help me get out of this relationship/marriage, Lord. Thank You in advance for what You are going to do in my life, for answering my prayer. Amen.

"A PRAYER for any occasion"
Thank You, Lord, for allowing us to see another day. Some people who were living yesterday, died last night. You've given all of us yet another chance to experience life on earth again today. You've bided us more time to get *rightful* living *right*. No matter what our problems, we know that You will help us get through them. Show us how to interact with others, without letting our own problems and emotions get in the way. We need Your guidance and direction on how to love our neighbors as ourselves. We pray for others around the world; specifically, those individuals less fortunate. Continue to watch over all of us. Amen.

You've reached the end of the "Chaplain's Corner." I hope that you or someone you know has found one or more of these prayers helpful in praying about your circumstances.

"Wishing Upon a Star"

Star light,
star bright...
Watch over me tonight.
Protect me from harm.
In my mind,
God's *not* very far.
I wish upon a star.

"Father, Can You Hear Me?"

O God, *where art Thou*? I'm feeling such despair. I'm not good at handling this thing called "life" alone. I need You right now, Lord. Are You hiding Your face from me? Where are You, Lord? Please give me a sign that You are near. I ask this in Your name, Lord. Amen.

I often think about patients and people both inside and outside of these hospital walls, who are unable to communicate their needs and concerns. I wrote a poem about them. It has a simple title...

"Voiceless"

This poem
is for all of those patients and
people in general,
all around the world,
who have no voice.
Some of us *hear* you,
silently speaking out.
As you lay there
in hospital beds,
smiling through
the pain,
as your loved ones make decisions
about *you*,
without
your permission,
your consent...
a select few *hear* you.
We *get* it
as you voicelessly,
fight for your independence
and your dignity.
As you attempt to
exert your power with your distinct frowns
and sad eyes,
some of us *get* it...
We understand *you*.

Keep speaking out
with *all of your might*.
Put up a *fight*!
You matter,
ma'am or sir.
Helplessly trying
to express yourself,
frustratingly attempting
to tell us,
what you want
and need.
Some of us *hear* you,
as we stand there
in silence,
exerting ourselves through
God's power,
with the
ministry of presence,
and God's grace.
As you cry out
for help,
many of us *hear* you...
We've *been*
in your shoes.
You've been *crying out* in pain;
yet,
few know
what your *inner* struggle,
is all about.
Some of us *know*,
because
God has nudged us,
while in your presence.

We know to give you,
some *extra* loving care.
We know that,
your burdens
have gotten,
hard to bear.
We love you,
this we know.
Showing you,
through a loving touch.
Praying for you much.
We *hear* you,
the voiceless.
Your *silent* tears,
your *valid* fears...
These things have *not*,
gone unnoticed.
Fighting for your *life*,
avoiding *strife*.
You are watched over,
as you are elevated
to a *special* status...
The *voiceless*.
The *cared for*.
May you *silently soar*!

"A PRAYER for Girls and Women"

Lord,

We come to You today with humble hearts. As girls and women, we thank You for blessing us with beautiful faces and shapely bodies. You also blessed us with intelligence, ambition, poise, caring natures, and nurturing spirits. We are grateful!

At this time in history, many of us are thriving; yet others are struggling. Encourage us, Lord. We pray, Lord, that You not only guide our lives; but that, You also help us to empower and assist others (those females who need to see You through us most). We all need You, Lord. Help us, Lord. And please soften the hearts of more men; so that they are more respectful of us and more sensitive to our needs. Strengthen our boys and men, so that we can all co-exist in Your world, Lord.

Lord, we hear of domestic violence incidents, human trafficking epidemics, and sexual assault/Me Too scenarios that let us know that girls and women are being greatly abused and mistreated. Reverse these societal ills, please. Lord, hear our prayer.

Lord, so many women are suffering from illnesses; such as breast cancer and other terminal illnesses. Put in place more preventative measures and coping mechanisms. Heal those who have been recently diagnosed. Guide us to helpful resources so that we as girls and women are more informed about our bodies and warning signs of trouble. Lord, hear our prayer.

Lord, many women are single mothers supporting themselves and their children. Provide abundantly for them. Lord, hear our prayer.

Lord, show us the way to be positive role models for girls and women with low self-esteem. Provide us with the means to educate girls and women on dress code and proper etiquette. Lord, hear our prayer.

Lord, give us the resources to prepare girls and women for STEM careers where they are scarce, for their future roles as wives, and for their familial positions as mothers to their children. Lord, hear our prayer.

Lord, give us the right words to say to lead more girls and women to You, or back to You. Lord, hear our prayer.

We give thanks to You, Lord. Thank You for saving us from ourselves and our sins! *(Pause for reflection)*

Watch over Your girls and women. Watch over the males in Your world, Lord. *(Pause for reflection)*

Protect our children. Restore and strengthen family units in our Communities, Lord. *(Pause for reflection)*

Heal those individuals who are suffering and/or hurting. Watch over Your people, Lord. *(Pause for reflection)*

We strive to be more like You. Keep loving us, Lord. Amen.

HOPEFUL THOUGHTS

"Hope Floats"

What is hope?
Is God within this scope
of understanding?
He is behind
the bringing about
of something
or someone we desire.
So,
I must conclude that,
God is in the midst
of hope.
Stirring up the pot,
preparing to bring about an outcome.
It starts to boil until it bubbles over.
In the end,
it releases God's grace.
In every opportunity,
to our delight...
We can see God's face.

"If You Believe"

Times are hard
but if you believe,
you will survive.
He will help you up
when you fall,
if you just believe.
You can succeed,
if you only believe.
You can learn to love yourself,
if you believe.
All things are possible,
if you just believe.

"I'll Be Stronger than Before"

With God's help, I'll be stronger than before.
Through trials and tribulations, I grow.
Through mistakes, I learn.
Through fear, I change.
I wait patiently as God opens the door.
Uncertainty of not knowing what is beyond,
feeling anxiety more and more.
Surely I'll be stronger than before.
Future visions fill my mind.
Wherever You lead me, Lord, I shall follow.
And surely, I'll be stronger than before.
What is Your plan with me, O Lord?
I can sense changes coming on.
Save me from this madness, Lord.
I'll be stronger than before.
Decisions, preparations, rearrangements…
I wait for the outcome.
Right now all I know is,
I'll be stronger than before.
Guide me, teach me, mold me, and carry me.
With You, Lord...
I'll be stronger than before.
When I see Your footprints,
I know that
I'll be stronger than before.

Trial Sermon - Rockwell AME Zion Church, Charlotte, NC [March 15, 2017]
Preacher: Rev. Vickie L. Hughes
Psalm 30:1-5NRSV, "Can There Be Joy in the Midst of Suffering?"

Tonight, I'd like to explore a question with all of you. Can there be *joy* in the *midst* of *suffering?*

A Chinese Proverb declares that *"One joy scatters a hundred griefs."* I believe that *one joy* to be *"Jesus."* Despite our *suffering*, we can *still* hold on to *hope* and find *joy*.

We *all* suffer in different ways… *Physical* pain, *Mental health* challenges, *Emotional* pain while grieving the loss of loved ones, *Financial* hardships, *Job* loss, *Relationship* challenges. You *name* it, we *may* go *through* it. None of us *suffer* in vain. *Sometimes*, God chooses to test good people, not as a punishment, but to see *just* how strong their *faith* is.

Rev. Dr. Martin Luther King, Jr. talked of a different type of suffering… *"unearned/unmerited"* suffering. He felt that *often* we suffer simply because we are *flawed*, *imperfect* human beings… We *sin*; yet, this type of *suffering* is redemptive. Jesus *died* on that cross for *us*, so we are *saved* no matter what. *(Are you with me?)*

I came here tonight to tell you that… *Whatever* you are going *through*, Jesus *grieves* and *suffers* with you. There is a *purpose* for *everything* that happens to you. You *will* see brighter days.

Psalm 30, Verse 5 *really* speaks to me. What may puzzle *some* people is how *weeping* and *joy* are in the *same* sentence in that verse. How is *that* possible, to feel *sad*, *bad*, or *mad*, yet find *joy* in all of *that*? *(End of intro)*

David wrote Psalm 30 as a Prayer of Thanksgiving, rather than a Psalm of Lament. He was grateful to God for saving his life, and getting him back on track! He'd made a mess of his life, by getting involved with Bathsheba. But *that's* a story for *another* time! *("Hood" people will understand that favorite saying [a Hood Theological Seminary inside joke].)*

There are others in the Bible who, *unlike* David, endured *extreme* suffering, hardship, and pain, for various reasons; no fault of *their* own… And God was *always* there for *them*.

Has *anyone* in here *ever* experienced great *loss*? Let me remind you about *Job*, who was *wealthy* like our *modern-day* Oprah. Job was well-respected by others and had strong faith in God. While Job was enjoying life, the devil was wandering around looking for his next victim. He is *always* up to something. He was looking for *weak* people! One day, God agreed to *allow* the devil to *test* Job, in order to prove Job's steadfast faith in God.

Over the years, Job lost *everything* he *had*... His *animals* that were his means of income, his servants were *killed*, his children *died* in a natural disaster, his *health* declined, and his *physical appearance* was *unsightly*. Through it *all*, Job's wife and his friends became angry and *turned* on God. They encouraged Job to *do the same* and *betrayed* him, when he *wouldn't*. Job was *distraught*; yet he didn't *curse* God like *some* people *would have. (Can I get a witness?)* We've *all* had a *Job* experience, where we've lost *something* or *someone*... Your *relationship*, your *car*, your *house*, your *job*, or your *health*. Heck, *some of us* in *here* are *Job* right now! Or a *female* version of *Job*!

Job almost *lost* his will to live at *one* point; but, *one* day he *remembered* God's *goodness*. He restored his faith and *prayed* to God for help! After Job prayed for his wife and friends, God blessed Job again; *this* time with *two* times what he'd *previously* had.

If you're *facing* loss, *know* that God *can* restore. You *can* find *joy* in *that* possibility. Job suffered for *many* years; yet, he found *joy* when God *rewarded* him for his faith during his *hard* times. Your faith can *never* waver! Many trials end in triumphs, if you can just *hold on* and *wait them out*!

Job's *suffering* story was a *forerunner* to the *Jesus* narrative of suffering. We *all know that*, the person who endured the *most suffering ever* on this earth, was *Jesus. (Can I get a witness?)*

Jesus was *taunted, teased, bullied, rejected, abused, tortured, and crucified.* He was *ignored* and *mistreated,* because *many* did not *know* or *understand* who He *truly* was. He endured *extreme* suffering during His lifetime, until the very end of His life when He called out, *"It is finished."*

During *Jesus's* lifetime while dealing with His *own* troubles, He *cared for* and *wept for* us. *"Jesus wept"* is the *shortest* verse in the Bible.

Many people have *misunderstood* that verse *(Are you with me?)*… Jesus *wasn't* weeping over the loss of Lazarus. *Why* would Jesus *do that*? Jesus *knew* that He was about to *raise* Lazarus from the dead and that *Lazarus* was about to *walk* through town in front of *all* of the people. Jesus *wept* because He *looked over* at *Mary, Martha,* and their *friends*; witnessed them *grieving*; and that *saddened* Him, so He *wept*. Jesus *always* thinks of *us* and desires to *help* us.

Before Jesus faced His suffering and death on that cross, He *agonized* over the state of *all* of humanity the night before He died. Two of the four Gospels focus more on the *"suffering," human* side of *Jesus*. While in the Garden of Gethsemane, He *truly* wasn't thinking about *Himself*… Jesus *knew* that His crucifixion was forthcoming; yet He *prayed fervently* asking *God* if humanity's *sins* could be *forgiven any other way*. We all know *that* answer… God's answer was *"No."*

God came to earth as Jesus. His crucifixion and resurrection paid the price for *all* of humanity's sins. Jesus was *God* in the midst of the people. He experienced their *problems* with them and *felt* their pain. We do *not* suffer alone… *Never have, never will!* God has *always* been here for us.

God *was not/is not* the orchestrator of all of this *evil* and *sin* in our world. We *know* that God didn't *abandon* Jesus while on *that cross*, so He *surely* has *not* forgotten about *us*. Trust that He continues to *want* to help us *fix* our world.

Jesus *is* the reason *why* we can find *joy* in the *midst* of our *suffering*. Our *suffering* is buried *in* and *with* Jesus's suffering… Hearing *that* should give us *comfort*.

Jesus is not physically here on earth any longer, but is with us *always*, through the Holy Spirit that He sent to us after He died. Jesus died for us because God wanted us to be *alright*… To be able to face *brighter* tomorrows. And we *can*! Jesus died for us, so that we can *endure* and *hope* during our various trials. God is *always* with us. He *suffers* with us. He *cries* with us. Our individual *and* collective pain, *pains* Him.

Often, people go through things because God has *chosen* to change their paths or to teach them a specific lesson. During your trials, as *painful* as they may *seem… Wait them out* and see what God *might* be doing *in* and *with* your life. All of us have options when we experience trials and tribulations. You can either have a *"Woe is me"* attitude, or one that says, *"I will make it!"* You can *allow* your suffering to *defeat* you, or you can *allow* God to *guide* you. You *can* find *joy* in the midst of suffering, if you *trust* and *believe* in God; *pray* to Him for *help*, *comfort*, and/or *healing*.

We all know that we are losing *too many young people* to suicide, usually resulting from aftereffects of someone's bullying efforts. *Adults*, it is *our* responsibility to teach these young people some *coping* skills!

To the *youth* and *young adults* in here *tonight*, I say to you… There is *nothing* in this world that you *can't* handle! I know some people who have overcome handicaps or extreme childhood traumas. If you ever find yourself, crying yourself to sleep at night… Know that *God* is there *with* you. If you've decided that your life is *so* messed up that it's not worth living anymore... *Trust* God and *ask* Him for *help*. Cry out *Jesus's* name. In your moment of *desperation*, Jesus will *tell* you that *your* life is *worth* living, that *you matter*, and that He has a *purpose* for your life. Rest, assured that He will *work things out* on your behalf. Romans 8:28 *assures* all of us of *that promise*. God *will* bring you joy in the morning. And things will begin to *change* for the *better*, in your life.

(Getting ready for the start of my 'hoop!' Wait for it…)

Know that God is *everywhere*, *all* of the time… Jesus is with *each* and *every* one of us, *every day and night* of our lives. He *suffered* while here on earth; He *suffered* with our ancestors; and He also *suffers* with us *today*. Jesus *knows* what we are going through and He goes through things *with* us.

There are *people* in here *tonight*, who have lost *children* or other loved ones to murders, substance abuse, or death from various physical illnesses. *Know* that *Jesus* will *always* be here with you, as you *continue* to grieve.

Jesus *knows* that many individuals come to Church while in *tremendous* physical pain, most Sundays; yet they come to *worship and praise* Him *anyhow*.

Jesus *knows* that *many* women are experiencing domestic violence; that *many* youth are troubled; that *numerous* households are dysfunctional; and that *many* families are homeless.

Jesus *knows* who is *currently* seeking employment; who has *minimal* food at home to eat; and which parents/caregivers are *struggling* to make ends meet. *Of course,* these individuals need to *care for* their families.

Jesus *knows*!

Know that *Jesus* overcame His *trials* and *tribulations*.

After He *died*…

He *rose*!

He was *resurrected*!

He *got up*...

And He *started a new life*! *(Pause and let that sink in!)*

God *helps* you if you *ask*... God *comforts* you when you *need* Him... And God *loves* you no matter *what*. He *continuously* grants you *favor*. *Know this*... You may *weep* at night, but *joy* comes in the morning. *Trust God* and *embrace Jesus*! Jesus *travels* your journey *with* you and *carries* you when He *needs* to do so.

Yes, there *can*, be *joy*, in the *midst* of *suffering*. *(Coming to a close! Ooh wee, I'm almost finished...Whew!)*

Once, an anonymous author *boldly* stated... "Joy is a flower that blooms when *you* do." I believe that you *bloom*, when you get to know Jesus *intimately*. Knowing Jesus *gives* you *hope*! Jesus will *lead* you *through* troubled waters; so that you can *have* or *continue* to *have*, a *joyous* life.

Shirley Caesar has a song called, *"This Joy I Have."* Now, I don't want to run you *out of here*, so I *won't* be *singing* it *tonight*. *(laughter erupts)* But I hope that you all *leave here*, thinking of *these* words... "This joy I have, the world didn't give it to me... Well, Shirley... What is this that you have and who gave it to ya? Nobody but Jesus... Jesus, nobody but Jesus! He gave it to me; oh yes, He did! This joy that I have... Jesus, He gave it to me. Nobody but Jesus... Jesus! I dare you to try Him. He's alright!" *That* song is *amazing*! Thank You, *Jesus*, for *giving* us *joy*! Amen.

[All italicized/emphasized words, questions, and thoughts have been left in this printed sermon just for fun.]

"SCARS"

I encourage you to reach for the stars;
it matters not your number of scars.
Expose them;
you can help *somebody*.
On your upward climb,
reach down
and grab *somebody's* hand.
We all know,
there are *hurting* people in our land.
Scars have shaped you into,
who you are.
Your destiny awaits.
It's not very far!
Through past pain,
the end result was much gain.
We get older each day.
We learn that all people
have been through *something*.
Our suffering
is never experienced in vain.
Survival is achievable;
seek guidance and learn the way.
Scars...
They *mold* us.
Shaping us into stronger stock.
Whatever your experience,
you can never turn back the clock.
You went through your ordeal.
No matter how that trial made you feel,
you *survived*.

Whenever it was over,
you may have felt *shame*.
So, into the sand you dived,
to hide yourself from the world.
Your emotions swirled
as you continued to consider,
the impact of your setback.
Then,
God *gifted* you
with a plan of attack.
You fought your way to the surface.
It was your Savior who *got you through*.

Scars,
remind us of *where we've been*.
They reveal a path of growth.
Some of them,
teach us about sin and redemption.
A few prompt us to forgive,
because others have hurt us.
Many of our lessons were learned,
the hard way.
We tried to get back on our feet...
After getting into mess after mess,
that was no small feat.
Feeling the heat,
as we crashed and burned;
immediately,
God's forgiving nature was remembered.
Through Jesus,
it had been earned.
Remembering my tears,
collected in jars...

I can feel them
rolling down my cheeks,
as if I shed them yesterday.
They solidified my hurt.
Looking back,
I know that
they represented and defined,
the nature of my resulting scars.

"MY Quote to Live by"

"Other people's blessings are theirs to claim and *my* blessings are *mine* to embrace/keep. No one's blessings are the same. God blesses in His own time, based on what I need and what will bless *me* and those around *me*, when the time is right. *My* blessings will come to *me* when God feels that the world and I need them most. *My* blessings are coming...
I'm excitedly waiting for them!"

Worship Service Sermon - Hood Theological Seminary, Salisbury, NC [Fall 2017]
Preacher: Rev. Vickie L. Hughes
John 17:9-19NRSV, "A Hedge of Protection"

If you would, please... I'd like for each of you to imagine being one of the 11 disciples who had just shared and finished The Last Supper with your Minister, Preacher, Teacher, Mentor, and Friend. You don't know what to think, or how to feel about Him going away forever. You're feeling anxious, sad, and confused; because Jesus has told you that He will soon, be going away... You don't know if and when, you'll ever see Him again. You've just spent 3 years with Jesus, interacting with Him every day. He's been like a brother to you, so you know you'll miss Him. You will most likely feel lost without Him. You are in disbelief and could use comforting and some direction. You wonder... "How will I survive without You, Lord?" *(End of Intro)*

We can all relate to that scenario in our own ways, whether we are preparing for others' departures or our own. We've all had these tender moments with others at some point in our lives, whether they were relatives or friends. Have you ever left loved ones behind when you moved, or watched loved ones die? Were you anxious or calm? Were you wondering what life would be like without those people, or were they wondering if they would ever see you again? Whenever we've experienced breakups/divorces or witnessed loved ones die slowly from terminal illnesses... We've all had to prepare for some sort of departure. We might wonder how we will survive as single parents, who will help us pay our bills, or who we will talk to about personal things once our loved one is gone. Those dying of cancer may have time to spend with loved ones, reminisce about past memories, give future instructions to spouses or advice to minor children, and say goodbye. Those leaving us may even offer us, words of consolation. Just think about your emotions at times like these. I see you, as an emotional wreck... I know, because I've been there. Truthfully, the saying, *"Until we meet again,"* if that is to ever happen; is truly a scary thought! I hope you'll be okay. Are you covered? Has God given you that hedge of protection that you so desperately need?

As we relate to today's text… Think again of being in Jesus's presence. Here Jesus is, praying for you, a disciple; all the while knowing that He will die soon at the hands of His enemies. Remaining calm while you're anxious, Jesus prays on your behalf while trying to comfort you; reassure you of your bright future; and promise His everlasting presence in your life. He assures you that you will be just fine. How *humbling* is that!

On the night before He was crucified, Jesus could have been anywhere, doing anything. He could have been praying, begging, and pleading for His life for several hours. Instead, we read in the Gospels that Jesus washed His disciples' feet, broke bread with them, and prayed for them. In His prayer, Jesus only spent the first few verses with a focus on Himself, and that was only to remind God that He had done all that God had assigned Him to do, while here on earth. The rest of this prayer was Jesus praying for His current disciples and those to come. He spent some of His last hours on earth, praying for us!

These verses that were read today, are part of Jesus's Farewell Discourse. John 17:1-26 is known as Jesus's *High Priestly Prayer*, a prayer for those who followed Jesus. He prays this prayer in front of His disciples shortly after The Last Supper. During this Prayer, Jesus considers His destiny/legacy after His death in verses 1-5; His relationship with His 11 disciples and other followers, in verses 6-19; and His hope for all people as well as those who will follow Him for years to come, in verses 20-26.

Today, I am focusing on verses 9-19, a small part of this powerful prayer. The verses focus on eleven of the 12 disciples who had walked with Him; one of His disciples had already betrayed Him. They needed *"a hedge of protection,"* so that they would press on; no matter what they faced. Some ministered for years; but were constantly persecuted. Some were imprisoned like Peter, who was also eventually crucified.

Jesus selflessly considers the disciples' safety from persecution and the world's sin, so He speaks to God on their behalves. Jesus asked God to bond disciples together, sanctify them, and then protect them; since they were truly not of this world. They were to be set apart and made holy (the true meaning of the Greek word, "Hagiazo (*Hag-E-O*)," or sanctification), so that God could use them for His glory in furthering/bettering His Kingdom.

Jesus speaks about protection, in verses 11, 12, 15, and 18. He specifically refers to His disciples called out for Ministry… In today's world, that's *us*! Remember Martin Luther King, Jr., Nelson Mandela, Mother Theresa, and Oscar Romero. Knowing what God would call His disciples to do, Jesus prayed that we would be protected in our endeavors… Pastoring; Evangelizing; Ministering; Preaching; Counseling; Teaching; and Sowing. Jesus let His disciples know, that we are always covered no matter what we face.

Jesus knew then that His disciples would suffer, because He was asking them/giving them permission to do all that He had done and *He'd* suffered during His ministry. He merely asked God to give them/us/you, the same covering of protection that *He* was given while navigating the world. He was protecting us from being negatively affected by the sins of the world.

Think about your own Christian walks. Ask yourself, *"Am I covered with God's hedge of protection?"* Jesus prayed for His believers/followers who were not of the world, to be protected. If we are out here in the world doing ungodly things... Well, we're on our own! If we are over *here* and God has called us to be over *there*... We know we are not where we're supposed to be. God's protection doesn't *exactly* cover that! Now, when we are about God's business, Jesus ensured that we are covered by praying for our protection, before He departed this earth (though that does not mean that we will never have trouble, it means that we as Christians are watched over by the Holy One)...

Jesus could have prayed for anything concerning His disciples and followers, but He chose to do what any good parent would do. He prayed that His family would be protected while He is gone. And, Jesus wanted His disciples firmly rooted in their faith. Jesus watched out for us!

God expects us to live like Christ and also, to engage in the same type of actions, like making sure that everyone is treated equally; comforting the sick and shut-in; loving all people; advocating for oppressed groups; teaching individuals to be humble and fair; and preaching about God. If we are not out here in the world trying to better God's Kingdom, can we truly expect to be protected with God's hedge of protection?

We will suffer various things while here on earth (i.e. persecution for being Christians, illnesses, financial woes); and of course, that's Bad News. The Good News is that Jesus ensured our protection when we are living like Him and living right, because all things work together for those who love Him. Things may seem bleak, but things can change for the better in an instant. Because we as Christians have been given this hedge of protection that I'm referring to, we are expected to take the time to bring others to Christ. His hedge of protection is limitless; it extends to all who desire it. It is our responsibility to work in God's Kingdom effectively, which means to be good disciples. We are rewarded when we are good disciples, spread the Good News about Christ, and convert others to discipleship. Isn't that Good News?

Jesus let us know, that He would always be our Advocates. We read that in John 17:1-26; we can personalize it further, in verses 9-19. Because of Jesus's advocacy and God's protection, we can face all of our tomorrows. The Great Commission we read about in Matthew 28 tells us that we are to go out and be active disciples, no matter what... And we are protected! We're covered! God has our backs.

We need to understand and appreciate what Jesus said and did for us! He prayed for us, that we would be taken care of after He left! We must spread the Good News that Jesus died for us so that we can lead good lives and that we are promised salvation! Our protection was provided to us when we decided to believe in Jesus. The Good News shortly after Christ was resurrected, was that His disciples turned Apostles, were able to win over many souls to Christ; they fueled the Christianity movement. The Good News now is that God doesn't just throw us to the wolves when we get saved! Getting saved, means that we are truly saved! We are given an assurance of grace, a certain degree of protection in life, and the promise of salvation after death. Some of us accepted our calls into ministry; we are supposed to boldly call on the Holy Spirit and trust God completely. We can't hesitate to go beyond the four walls of our Churches, spread the Gospel, and bring others to Christ. The Good News brings us face-to-face with salvation. Others need to know this!

Charles "Chuck" Colson went to prison years ago, for his involvement in the Watergate/Nixon scandal. While in prison, he was converted to Christianity. He once said, "Men will give their lives for something they believe to be true—they will never give their lives for something they know to be false."

You know that…
• Jesus prayed for you in what should have been His moment of desperation, the night before His death.
• Jesus, thinking of His disciples/followers, asked God to protect them/us from harm as we live out our lives as Christian disciples.
• Jesus asked God to make you holy, so that you are living rightly and glorifying/exalting God/Jesus/Holy Spirit.
• Jesus asks you now to believe in Him, to trust Him, and to follow Him.

You are protected from the evil one and from evil, in the way that God chooses to protect you. You accepted Christ, so you are saved. Jesus has provided us with *"a hedge of protection,"* through the Father. So, disciple… Have no fear and trust God, because you are covered! Now that doesn't mean that you will never have a problem or face trials and tribulations. It means that God is with you and watches over you, whenever you go through something. Other times, having that hedge of protection over your life could mean a diversion from danger or harm. Again, God has not given us a spirit of fear. We are called to be disciples to others. Nothing should stop us! Today, humanity needs our help. Go out into the world, spread the Good News, and bring lost souls to Christ. And when you do, heaven will eventually be your resting place, as well as theirs. *Go run tell that!* Amen.

AWESTRUCK MOMENTS

"I Keep Finding God"

Clouds.
The perfect imprints;
I see the Lord's footprints,
those that often carry me.
My "*Embedded Theology*"
for all to see.
Yes, He watches over me.
Uniquely designed is this
vast nature scene.
This gaze
blows my mind.
Often a clear vision
to Heaven.
Pieces of a puzzle,
different shapes formed
as they surround
the entrance.
I know for a fact,
that He is there.

I see Him in other people
and in the center of circumstances.
He shows up
in the quietness of a room,
He also finds us
in all of our busyness
and noise.
He sits with us
in the midst of our messes.
Changing our lives for the better,
is something He addresses.

He gets deep into our lives
and opens His arms so wide.
When in crisis mode,
from Him we cannot hide.
He is there for us.
He's invisible;
Yet, He's present.
He's effervescent!

I keep finding God
in familiar places,
as I experience Him differently.
I find Him in the miracles of life.
He is present in the light
and in the dark.
I find Him
in unforeseen circumstances,
when He gives others
their second chances.
Something I've discovered
in my spoken and written words,
is that...
I keep finding God in me.
I keep finding God.
As you turn these pages,
I hope and pray that
it will be God you'll see.

"All Things Spiritual"

As I look out of
the window,
I am gazing...
I see that,
our bright sun
is no longer blazin'.
Today,
the sky is mighty dreary.
As I wait for
the sun's brightness again,
I remember when...
I traveled to faraway places.
I leaped into the unknown.
I was young then.
Oh how I've grown!
Today,
the sun is hidden;
yet,
my happiness,
is *not* forbidden.
Searching for,
hoping for...
That *one* door!
I am leaning into myself,
expecting *more*.
Each day,
more discoveries come.
With each new day,
I blossom some.
Self-awareness takes me,
inside of myself.

I find hidden pieces of "*me*,"
on a shelf.

I now realize that,
I *am* the sun.
I can remove my veil
and come out anytime.
My very "*being*" sublime,
as my transformation occurs...
From chrysalis to butterfly.
With my evolutionary change,
my beauty transcends all.
I now fly high in the sky.

"The Ocean's Mystique, God's Creation"

As I sit at the window,
I hear the wind blow.
I look out at the ocean,
stretching miles beyond.
I see the waves so white,
rushing toward me.
I wonder about the ocean's mystery.
Ripples of motion.
What lies beneath this ocean?
Creations of God.
Salmon, bass, whales, and ling cod.
Ships traveling the length
of this aesthetic beauty,
if only to fulfill their duty.
Seagulls fly over to protect this territory,
acting like kings of the ocean.
At the same time,
the whales seek control
as they wallow in their glory.
The sand holds treasures -
the rocks and seashells represent,
some of life's pleasures.
As I sit at the window,
my eyes clue me in
to the ocean's mystique.
I realize that this creation
is truly unique.

(This poem was written in 1991, while vacationing in Newport, Oregon. God's creations have never ceased to amaze me. Any ocean/beach is a favorite place of mine, because as I gaze out into the ocean from a window or while sitting/standing outside breathing in fresh air… I find God there *each and every time.* It seems like heaven. God is everywhere in the vast space around me and beyond [the ocean, the sand, the clouds, and the sky]. He always speaks to me with a quiet whisper, as I take in His greatness and what He desires me to experience, observe, and know.)

"That Day"

That day I shed a few tears;
I actually had to wipe them away.
My voice cracked as I whispered,
some endearing words.
None clear as
the chills of birds.
Yet, her friends understood me,
Father God,
I was there representing thee.
I stood across from these three friends,
as they faced their fears.
They were there comforting their friend,
a hospital patient
who was actively dying.
They stood at bedside,
genuinely crying.
We prayed together.
Memories of their dear friend were
etched in their minds forever.
Never to be forgotten... Ever.
This patient was loved
and wished the best,
that God would ease her pain
and that,
she would not suffer long.
We were wrong.
We flunked that test.
The dying quest.
How long will the agony persist?
God is in control
in dying situations.

Patience controls
as the soul prepares to ascend,
way above the sun.
This patient did not breathe her last,
for six more hours.
Unfortunately,
pain devours.
Her friends stood by,
reminiscing about the past.
Their friend had declined fast;
yet,
she kept hanging on.
They were aghast!
It seemed as if their long-time friend
wanted to hang on for them.
Love's cherubim.
This was no con.
She was not ready to let go.
This patient loved her friends so.
I shed a few more tears when we hugged
and huddled later.
I can't say that I'm a waiter.
I stood there with them anyway.

Soon,
it would be a new day.
Then, there would be a new tune.
Hymns of promise.
Sorrow, grief, bliss.
How had we ended up like this?
Well, I do know indeed.
Our circle was what,
this patient needed.

We'd gathered together to begin
to grieve.
God bonded us further,
because we were the ones
who will always believe.
Tears flowed,
seeds sowed.
Heaven awaited our patient.
She knew that
it was God-sent.
She seemed ready,
then she clung to us.
At one point
as she heard
our comforting words,
her face lit up.
Runneth over my cup.
We had more to offer this patient...
A silent covenant between other females.
Biblical tales of Jesus,
darting around.
There were times when
we just gazed at each other.
The Holy Spirit does hover.
This patient passed away that day.
Sadness filled the atmosphere.
That's all I can say.

REFLECTIONS

"SOUL Reflection"

Reflection...
Gazing forward!
My past
often absurd.
My soul *cries out*.

My spirit *soars*!
Thankful for my blessings,
as well as
my lessons learned.
Curses *burned*.

Plunging into the sea of hope,
with my faith I will elope.
Shining brightly as a *beacon*...
Ordained Deacon!

Swimming away from the shore,
the unfamiliar becoming
a part of me
more and more.
The world's *deflection*...
My current
theological reflection.
Digging deeper,
getting richer.
Meaning and gleaning.

The moon shimmers
over the rippling waters,
in the still of the night.
As the dawn breaks,
the sun *shines brightly.*
My raft protects me,
as I keep drifting
further away.
I am in this place;
I can *no longer
hide* my *face.*
Shall I dock here
and stay,
or continue on my way?

Clear vision,
sightly gazes.
I do not
travel this path alone.
I realize now that,
I have not taken this reflection lightly.

"Morning Reflection"

Ask yourself... "Am I in my God-ordained position (i.e. location, job, city of residence, level of maturity, educational attainment, professional/personal achievements, marriage or singleness, ministerial assignment, field of study, role model status, leader or follower)? Am I where I'm supposed to be? Am I doing what pleases God? What have I accomplished with what I've been given? Are my strongest gifts shining through, for all to see and soak in?" Discern your destiny and get yourself in position for further greatness!"

Heading down the road... A road less traveled and a place where God meets humanity; He speaks through me as we travel on life's journey together in a mighty way...

"I am one of God's called, ministering to hurting persons, those who have been forgotten and tossed aside, and/or those who may wonder if God still exists. I appear at and in various places hoping to make evident the presence of God, wherever I go. He loves us so! If I can give a person a glimmer of hope or a bit of faith, I have allowed that person to see God so that his/her journey will be brighter. I'll move on traveling through time to my next destination/assignment, hoping that God is pleased with me. That's what matters most - Have I done what God wanted me to accomplish that day? Did I obey Him? Have I heard from Him and spoken His words to another in the right way? Did I minister to this or that person in the proper manner? These things I pray."

"MY 'thinking about thinking' moment"

Biblical application +
Intellectual aptitude +
Intuitive thought +
Diverse mindset +
Outside-the-box perspective +
Prophetic reflection =
Social justice proaction

"Lifting the Veil"

Jesus walked this earth for 33 years and had His active Ministry for 3 years. Yet, He was *"invisibly invisible."* No one knew who He really was. He told people who He was, but people had this certain image of Him/belief about Him. They had this preconceived notion that He was ordinary, not extraordinary. They believed Him to be perpetrating His greatness, His purpose. It wasn't until He was gone when most people really got to know Him. He'd been *invisibly invisible*.

We really need to stop thinking that we "*know*" people. Often, we just know them on the surface. We don't know where they've come from, what they've been through, how they've survived, or what they've learned and the wisdom that they can teach us... We haven't taken the time to get to know them; instead, we've formed opinions based on how someone appears to us or so we think. We miss out on life that way! And we never know who is suffering silently as outcasts... Those rejected by society! Just think how many people wished they'd gotten to know Jesus before He was crucified. Each day and night for 3 years, He'd imparted Godly wisdom, performed divine miracles, did kind acts, and exhibited loving behavior. Why miss out on all of that?

Each day, we make a choice to either accept a person, or reject that person. Is your rejection justified? Have you learned or experienced enough about that person, to have formed an opinion; whether good or bad?

"Those Final Moments..."

When I'm in a hospital room
with an actively dying patient,
whether loved ones are there or not...
I find myself in sacred space. *(I start to reflect.)*
As I stand or sit with a patient,
I intently watch
his/her perfectly-shaped face.
So many details;
yet, a different expression can be found
on each patient's face.
A patient is often speaking
without making a sound.
Sometimes a patient looks to be
in agonizing pain.
Another patient may look fearful,
scared of the "*dying*" part...
Fearing the unknown, the end.
Still another patient
has a peaceful presence
on his/her face.
It seems as if
there may already be present,
a glimpse of heaven...
Already gone to glory,
experiencing a realm
somewhere up above,
wanting no part of coming back.
This place he/she has found

in his/her final existence,
is one of unfamiliarity to me.
My imagination brings clear focus… I am in the room,
toning down my full of life
and joyful aura.
I am solemn for now,
as I empathize
with my fellow being;
I adjust my demeanor
to be present in those final moments.
I am whispering softly.
I am observing surroundings.
I am pondering
the perfectness
of the room's conditions.
I am wondering about
the patient's mindset...
A penny for 'your thoughts.'
I am praying within myself,
asking God to assist me with
soft understanding utterances
and loving gestures.
I am assuring my patient that,
God is with him/her.
There could be gasped words
or excited utterances,
coming from my patient's mouth.
Perhaps I am witnessing,
silence and blank stares.
I am here.

I am asking God to ease the pain,
to lessen it or to take it away.
Sometimes I may even
beg my spiritual Father,
to be there in a mighty way
and assist my patient
with the transition.
There are times when
I am sharing dying moments
of a patient with family members
or friends.
Other times,
it is just the patient and me,
existing in the room's silence...
Just waiting,
agonizing over the slowly passing time.
Feeling the potential of death,
as it comes knocking.
Experiencing the dim darkness,
that fills the room...
It lingers long.
A patient's breathing may be raspy,
like the wind.
Time can tick away,
when I stay...

Comforting, experiencing,
being.
My mind may wander
for a brief second,
as I consider the value of life...
So precious,
so lived.
I may wonder and hope that
I am with a patient who
has lived a full life.
I think of the ups and downs
of our "*every days.*"
I envision this patient's happiness
and quickly dismiss the sadness.
Perhaps this patient's existence
has been consumed with madness.
Whatever the story,
I want to be here in this room
as he/she is being groomed for glory.
I am with this patient
in a current sacred space.
I have consciously chosen
to cherish these final moments.
I caress arms or hands.
I watch every movement.
I learn about endurance.
I love tenderly.
I am present,
yet self-aware;
in those final moments...

"WISDOM Quotes"

"I invite *you* to take up *that* cross and do something *mind-blowing* with it!"

"I'd rather follow in God's footsteps, than yours."

"Sometimes you need to flaunt God's blessings so that people know *exactly* what He can do in people's lives."

"Who am I? Who am I to not acknowledge God, who created the universe? Who am I to try to play God, by elevating myself in my mind and acting accordingly? Who am I to bypass the hierarchical order that God put in place? I must respect living creatures that God has entrusted to my care. It is imperative that I value other peoples' lives as much as my own. And it is crucial that I worship and praise my Creator. I must learn my purpose and place on this earth, and in life. And then I must live out my purpose and contribute greatly to the world. Who am I? I am a child of the most High, God Himself."

"God keeps on blessing me, so that I can bless others. After all, that is my purpose on this earth... Yours too! Recognize God's grace, mercy, and love when He shows you favor. And do *yourself* a favor; pass on what God gives you."

"In all of your endeavors and interactions, allow God to use you. Shine bright like a diamond. Love your neighbor like you would want that person to love you. Exercise faith, spread love, and share hope."

"Are you ready to take the world by storm?!?! I know I am! It's *never too late* to show them what you got, and *what God can accomplish through you*. Ha! You ready? Ready, set... Go! Right now, right now." (smile)

"Enjoy your current view and circumstances. Only God knows where He's leading you next. Trust Him to get you where you need to go."

"While I have unconsciously been *set apart*, I have *subconsciously* attempted to fit in."

"In the Grand Scheme of Things"

In the grand scheme of things,
I exist.
In the midst of the crowd,
I stand.
I look around and view humanity.
I sense that some of these people
aren't very kind,
so I decide to erase them from my mind.
I search for those who,
I believe
would be a friend to me,
and to you… No matter what.
I find a few,
a few who display smiles on their faces,
who may have lived in
or traveled to distant places.
I look up and thank God
for blessing us with
the little bit of decency
of humankind,
we have left.

In the grand scheme of things,
I sense turmoil and unrest,
in some people.
Mental illness runs rampant
in our communities today.
It's a silent killer because…
Often we don't know who it has claimed,

until it is too late…
They have killed others,
and perhaps even themselves.
The stories end up all over the news.
Now I tell you,
that God has called me as one who,
is assigned the task of helping to,
help and heal people.
So, where do I begin?

In the grand scheme of things…
I talk to people,
and find out about their lives.
It is amazing that people
reach a comfort zone with me
that I could have never imagined.
I know that God did *that*!
And the spirit of discernment
He's gifted me with,
blows my mind.
I just need to remind myself,
to *always* listen to Him.
Here I am, once again,
on a quest searching for a person,
and/or a family to help.
I'm in the community,
promoting unity.

In the grand scheme of things,
I am concerned for humanity,
and specifically… My people!

I'm not sure how we've gone from slavery
where my people had to be strong;
through the Civil Rights Movement,
where my people had to *fight*;
to *now*...
Where some of my people have chosen to forget
our previous struggles,
and our trying past.
Back then,
there was a desire to survive, and to...
Overcome.
Now, anything goes,
and life doesn't seem to matter much,
for some people.
Sad as that is...
Truth be told!

In the grand scheme of things,
we matter!
Again,
I look around,
this time determined to find and see,
the good in people.
As someone called to care...
I'm prepared to save some lives,
even if I have to die...
You may ask why.
I know that God is working through me,
and it is not my nature to question His will and plan
for my life.
Whatever *shall be*, *shall be* for me.

In the grand scheme of things,
survival of the fittest no longer exists.
Those of us called must reach out and
help the underdog.
We must lift up others
and share our strength.
After all, this is God's Kingdom
that has gone astray.

In the grand scheme of things,
after we are long gone from this earth…
His Kingdom will remain, in *His* way.

GOD'S CALLING

"Displaying Empathy (Ode to Silence)"

God called *me* to *this*,
insecurities I must dismiss.
God desires that I be fully present,
when ministering to others.
He will push me and guide me...
God never smothers!
I'm trying to remain open
as I discover more and more
about *my* "stuff."

Enabler,
Controller...
Codependent on *something*.
Need,
Recognition,
Pride.
Oh no!

Humbling myself to allow God,
to fix *this* negativity.
Oh God,
turn this dysfunction of mine around.
I'm standing on shaky ground.
Wanting joy to be found,
I reach out,
I step in,
to help.
Hold me back, dear Lord.
Silence me,
free me of my desire

to fix,
to change,
to save.
Work through me to inspire.
Give me the words to save,
nudge me
when golden moments of silence
are required,
for You to work Your magic.
Show me the proper presence to have;
the right stance to display, to exhibit.

Father God,
hear my prayer...
When I'm with that someone who,
really needs You.
Guide me through the process,
to get that person to move;
taking personal, empowering action,
which could be for that individual,
a future improved life,
free from unnecessary strife.
Help me sit with others in pain.
I want their healing and comfort,
to be experienced as a gain.

A move, Lord, on Your part,
to change bitterness,
and another's heart.
Let me be that calming presence,
in others' lives...

Not exerting my control as a factor;
but, as I'm there with a person,
fully present,
sharing in his/her pain and suffering,
tender moments perhaps
bonding us together,
in his/her grief and loss,
at a time of dire need...
Let *Your* will be done *through* me.
Amen.

"Realness"

A *rarity*.
Wanting *clarity*,
loving me with *sincerity*.
A mass of confusion trying to find my place.
Settling further into Ministry,
I *seek out* His face.

Soaring *higher*,
where my spirit
will connect with others.
They will know
the *compassion* of my heart...
They will hear it.
God will speak *through* me.
Others shall *see*
His face.
Those who become familiar with Him,
will come to know His *grace*.

I step out on a limb,
exposing my vulnerability.
If I show you *me*,
you'll experience
my tenacity.

Clearer vision.
The focus
of my Ministry,
is *God's* decision.
I remain open...

Open to feel.
Willing to cry.
Hoping to just be...
Me!

About the Author

Rev. Vickie L. Hughes is an ordained AME Zion minister, preacher, speaker, poet/writer, and author of the book, *In the Still of the Night and the Wee Morning Hours... I Find God Everywhere.* She has worked in a Chaplain capacity (Resident and Intern) at three healthcare locations in the Southeast region, U.S.A. She also served as a Student Minister (Acting Pastor) of a Nondenominational Church for two years, while in Seminary. Vickie loves the Lord! Her professional career has also included work in nonprofit/territory management, law, and ministry. A proud graduate of Spelman College, she loves to inspire other females, both girls and women. In her spare time, Vickie loves to write, travel internationally, golf, listen to jazz, and paint. Currently, she resides in Tennessee.

Made in the USA
Monee, IL
17 February 2020